ALISTAIR FINDLAY is the author of
the shale oil communities of West L
two collections of poetry, *Sex, Deat*
Songs of John Knox (2006) and also edited a volume of football p———,
100 Favourite Scottish Football Poems (2007). He received a Scottish
Arts Council Writer's Bursary Award in 2007 to edit a critical anthology
of the poetry of Scottish Marxism and to complete the present volume
of poetry on social workers. He worked in front-line local authority
social work between 1973–2009, being among the first recruits to the
new 'generic' (one-door) social work profession which integrated all
four previous specialist services – probation, mental health, child care
and welfare. In 1970 he began a three year training course at Moray
House College, Edinburgh, then worked between 1973–5 as a social
worker for Falkirk Burgh, becoming a senior social worker there for
Central Region until 1977. He subsequently worked as a senior for
several Authorities, including Nottingham and Derbyshire and
Craigmillar in Edinburgh, and was Lothian Region's Coordinator for
Child Protection based in Edinburgh between 1984–91. He then joined
West Lothian as a senior in Broxburn and served as Children and
Families Practice Team Manager in Livingston between 1992–2009.
Active in NALGO, the local government trade union, he was Convenor
of the Lothian Region Social Work Shop Stewards Committee and
Branch Education Officer between 1982–6. He qualified CQSW with
distinction from Moray House in 1973, then took an MA in Applied
Social Studies (Bradford University, 1979), an honours degree in History
and Literature (Open University, 1993), a certificate with distinction in
Scottish Cultural Studies (Edinburgh University, 1995) and an MPhil with
distinction in Modern Poetry in English (Stirling University, 1999). He
retired from social work in February 2009 and lives in Bathgate.

To Sam,
Haud Furrit!
Best Regards

Dancing With Big Eunice

Alister Findlay

Missives from the frontline
of a fractured society

ALISTAIR FINDLAY

Luath Press Limited

EDINBURGH

www.luath.co.uk

First published 2010
Reprinted 2011
Reprinted 2013
Reprinted 2019

ISBN 978 1906817 28 2

The publisher acknowledges subsidy from

Scottish
Arts Council

towards the publication of this book.

The paper used in this book is recyclable. It is made from
low chlorine pulps produced in a low energy, low emissions manner
from renewable forests.

Printed and bound by
Bell & Bain Ltd., Glasgow

Typeset in 10.5pt Sabon by
3btype.com

for all those who ever gave,
got or didn't get
'a section 12'

Contents

Foreword

IF YOU EVER BELIEVED that anger is principally the prerogative of young men, prepare to think again.

Alistair Findlay admits he himself was surprised by the extent of the 'white knuckled rage' which threatened to engulf the creative process as he prepared to interpret a lifetime in social work service through his poetry.

Yet *Dancing With Big Eunice* emerges not as a rant so much as a wry, humour fuelled, wittily wrought homage to the front line troops who put so many fingers in the dam in order that the torrent of wrong headed policy initiatives fail to engulf more of the poor bloody citizenry than they do.

The black humour with which this work is laced fails to disguise the compassion lurking not so far beneath the superficial cynicism. Alistair Findlay may be a man at war with the bureaucratisation of his profession, but not with the human flotsam and jetsam of his trade; even when those bruised and battered by circumstance are not beyond passing a spot of GBH on to the services deployed to assist them.

It's not the social workers' job to weep, he observes in 'Outside', not their job to point the finger or criticise.

In fact, in this new collection, he does all three, and his readers should be properly grateful for a strong voice liberated by retirement.

Ruth Wishart

Poet's Preface

'BIG EUNICE' IS A metaphor for 'clients' – the people statutory social workers deal with; 'Dancing with' is a euphemism for what that often feels like; 'knee-trembling' is the politest term I could think of to suggest the loss of apprenticeship innocence – 'virginity' – I experienced as a raw recruit to the fledgling profession of 'generic' (one door) social work in my first job with Falkirk Burgh all of 36 years ago. One could add that 'Big Eunice' had few pretensions either about herself or me. The result:

> *Dancing with Big Eunice was,*
> *I must confess,*
> *a complete knee-trembling experience.*
>
> *She was a big girl, big and bonnie,*
> *big in tights, and without oany*

For readers who think this might be a rather disrespectful way to address those misfortunate enough to fall in the way of statutory local authority social work, they have obviously not heard some of the things clients call us. It is certainly not intended as disrespectful so much as honest, for the client population should not be confused with the self-effacing, shrinking violets depicted in social policy essays using terms like 'the deprived' or 'the poor', which might suggest a certain passive resignation in the face of Want, Ignorance, Disease. Such terms may apply in some cases, but by no means all. Resignation and victimhood may co-exist with sticking-up for oneself, physically and verbally. Indeed, an excess of sticking-up for oneself is sometimes what leads some into becoming social work clients in the first place, or their children.

My generation of social workers were told in the language of the times that we were called upon to both 'care and control' people who did not so much choose to work with us as were assigned for 'help': clients. Disrespect is in my view when the language of corporate capitalism is used in the welfare arena to describe relations between the state and its subjects in commodity terms: 'clients' are now addressed in policy documents as 'customers' or 'consumers of services', as though those placed on Probation could take their business elsewhere if they did not get on with the social workers allocated to them. Honesty is still the basis of respect, at least in front-line social work, the only kind I know about or care to defend. The misguided aspirations through which government ministers and their corporate management creatures offer up social workers as cure-alls for a fragmented society in fact ends, with media compliance, in social workers being held responsible for the misbehaviour of the people they are busy trying to help. This is as credible as holding the police responsible for the criminals they are trying to catch. It mis-states the actual role social work has in statute whereby compulsion can only follow when voluntary measures have been tried and shown to have failed – to the standards of a court.

Too much is now expected of social workers, who are neither clairvoyants nor 'engineers of the soul', as Stalin once called poets. Social workers are human beings often with the practical gift, and determination, to relate to people as human beings no matter how much some of them say they do not wish or need such help when courts and health professionals consider otherwise. The people referred to social workers are often emotionally damaged and alienated individuals but their behaviour is often not easily distinguishable from the oddly eccentric or the wayward and downtrodden for whom society, and society's laws, also exist. These are the daily conundrums which statutory social workers in particular face in their work which is partly why I have chosen to open this collection with a poem imagining Robert Burns as a social work 'client'. Forty years ago, Burns would not have come within a mile of the social work departments I worked in. Today, in the altered universe I have described, he very well might.

I was curious myself as to what would emerge when the Scottish Arts Council awarded me a writer's bursary to produce a collection of poems on social work and social workers after 35 odd years on the 'front-line' of Scottish local authority social work practice – a bang, a whimper, a Munch-like Scream, a Whitmanesque Yolp, all of the above? What I did not expect was the white-knuckled rage that erupted when I sat down before the metaphoric 'blank page'. Damned little 'thoughts recollected in tranquility' qua the Lake Poets poured out, more page after page of Loch Ness Monsters concerned not with clients or colleagues – the substance of social work – but its hidden architects, the Government, those Blairite-Brownite politicians and their creatures, the corporate managers, who have turned the welfare state from being a professionally led, vocationally informed, labour-intensive and clumsily humane calling into a budget-driven, top-down, short-term, market-orientated, pseudo-customised, super-market glossed guddle whose most pronounced achievements have to date been Sir Fred Goodwin and the War in Iraq. Why should we believe anything they say about child protection, education or crime? And I mean the whole modern, post-Thatcherite, political class.

But these are poems, not essays. They have no interest in debating statistics with a spokesperson for the Scottish Government. The truths they aim at are emotional and partial, not literal; grey, not black-and-white. Social work is about reaching human truths, awkwardly offered and not always easily arrived at through generations of poverty, injustice and social indifference, on society's part too. If these poems have a meaning beyond the occasion of their writing, then let it be this.

Alistair Findlay
Bathgate
January 2010

I am Robert Burns, headcase

I am Robert Burns, headcase,
trapped in the persona of a client,
on my way to a case conference
to discuss my unusual behaviours,
my drinking and liking of women,
my flouting gyte rules and conventions,

my long-suffering wife, my neighbours,
poor Holy Willie, whose religious beliefs
I discriminate against, my reprobate
companion, Tam O'Shanter, a blethering,
blustering, drunken blellum, I cannot
deny it, my sanity may lie in the balance,

my support for the French Revolution,
my purchase of cannons, my cadging
songs from the poor and unworthy,
my writing a poem to my newly born daughter,
unwed, like her mother, my laughing at
magistrates – I must be bipolar,

or else a Republican: I scream at the TV when
Blair gets a mention, there's some talk of
Sections, and someone called Asbos, I drink
in the Masons, I do not vote Labour, I may
turn Scots National, I fear I'm not normal
and perhaps never have been.

They Sit Waiting

They sit waiting
all the children I've ever taken
into care

for a parent to phone who has not
phoned for years
to tell them it has all been

a big mistake
their mother did not run off
to Leeds to marry a black man

or have five children to him
down there
and she'll have them all back

as soon as they stop wetting
the bed
or running off

or putting the home's cat
in the spin drier
as soon as it can be arranged

with the social worker
love you, love you all
love you lots

Rorie

Rorie never was very hard to spot, he'd be
the one wearing the Davy Crockett hat in

mid-summer, with cricket pads on, and
roaring at you across the road, joyful,

you should have been in Princes Street
the day, man: the Pussy wis Gorgeous!

His mother kept him in a cupboard till
he was three, but it wasn't till he rode

bikes down the sheer sides of bings
they realised he was mad, hooked-up

to the moon, but now he's fine so long as
he takes his medicine; his friend's Jack,

with the obsessive compulsive disorder,
who crams wood inside his tiny flat but if

you try moving it out he stays up all night
moving it back: he's mental, Rorie explains.

My First Adoption

My first adoption came three months
into the job
a woman had walked into the Infirmary
with a concealed pregnancy
gave birth, discharged herself
and went back to work, same day.

She lived with her parents
already had a child
was afraid her father would put her out
if he knew, especially
as she'd been drunk and could not
remember who the father was.

I wrote a letter to be opened
by the child when she was sixteen
assuming her new parents would tell her
she had been adopted, which began:
your mother wanted to keep you
but of your father little is known
except he was tall, had black hair
and blue eyes and perhaps came from Glasgow.

Charity

Charity, students I'd make write essays on,
their feelings, attitudes, beliefs, is it part,
or not, of the gift-relationship their tutors
keep harking on about, or a throw-back,
soup-kitchens, carding for lice, impetigo,
'Christmas Day in the Workhouse'?
Spell out how you'd spend twelve months
of the year saying 'No' to the underclass,
then, for one day only, open all the doors,
burst out the boxes for the poor! I remember
when, in 1973, a 15-pound turkey was donated
by a man who wanted to deliver it himself, yes,
to the chosen ones. It would not go in the oven,
the gas for which had been disconnected: discuss.

The new born baby

The new born baby was beautiful
asleep, cradled in the arms of a nurse,
her mother already gone from the hospital
to a drug den
her grandmother unwilling to come
from Carlisle, Pitlochry, Pittenweem
with her heart condition
the grandfather already in prison, dead
the subject of several previous convictions
against his own children

the child sleeps on, blissful,
unaware that someone like me has
already been phoned, care
arranged, and for the next four
years her mother will promise to change
her lifestyle, give up her addiction,
fail, try again, fail, then fight
to prevent her child's adoption by a
childless couple from Fife who will repair
most of the attachment problems

sleep on little one
you will have a brother, and a sister
whom you will find out about
when you are fourteen
and if you are resentful then I hope
it is not because you feel
more could have been done by
people like us

Poverty

Poverty has a smell, it's kind of dank
and musty, like you find gathered underneath
a leaky sink, in cramped, airless, overheated
rooms, bare floorboards, carpets strewn with
debris, but no toys, clutter, the junk that no one
bothers to remove for no one notices the stink,
the crunching under foot, or calls growling dogs
to heel, Alsatians mainly, that do quite literally
steal the food from out the mouths of babes,
whose sticky fingers point and stare and clamber
over strangers' knees and poke your hair like
you are long-lost cousins, not social workers
only there to inspect the premises, motivations,
a new lodger, lying on a chair, not yet wakened

Outside

you can tell nothing from the outside
I've learned, walking up the paths

of council schemes, tenements, private
dwellings, care homes, sheltered units

imposing Victorian facades, concrete
Sixties high-rise; some were full of love

or stank of pain, loneliness, humiliation;
some cried or raged or threatened while I

sat or stood on landings, hallways, often
not saying very much; not my job to weep,

point the finger at, criticise: best leave that
to those best qualified, the press, the public.

Inside

an old labourer, me, in winter weather
inside, hanging the pee, sweeping the floor

in plain view of the gaffer, an oaf, a fud
a forelock tugger, a repeater of phrases

cascading, day and daily, guffage, sent down
from the air-holes of the Scottish Executive

crud, geegaws, paper-hats, bells to ring and
whistles to blaw at the ear-holes of paupers

while I, in this *bourach* masquerading, this
beer-tent, do as I am able: I sweep the floor

Workers

Let me have about me workers who are fat
In the beam, but not in the head, well-fed
Natures that give cuddles or straight-talk
Without breaking stride, nor skulk nor hide
In their offices nor strut about in the shade of
Legalese, nor the fear of weak-kneed Seniors,
Afraid of God knows what, of making a mistake?
God, mistakes are what this world is made of,
Our daily bread, so let them not distort our
Features, we band of brothers, sisters, whose
Reward will not be found in headlines nor
Gongs hung round the necks of wasters. No!
We do our work in the people's cause, firing
Haylofts, saving maidens, slaying robber barons.

Parenting Classes

They've put me in charge of
parenting classes for Scotland.

Lesson number one:
this is a bairn, not a football.

Lesson number two:
a bottle does not mean

Coke, Bud or Newcastle.
Lesson number three:

above all, do not call
your first born *Placenta*.

The Senior Social Worker

The senior social worker lives
with a stick of dynamite up his arse
and the words 'clients-complaints-forms'
on a slow-burn towards the powder-kegs
of his balls, while his managers skulk
in their offices like Nazi war-criminals
waiting on phone-calls from the Institute
of Simon Wiesensthal.

He hears his team mutter darkly like
the crowds that gathered round the prison
cells of Myra Hindley, hoping this time
she will say Yes! It was me! But now
I've found God! Well, bollocks to that,
says the senior social worker, who'd
rather have sex with an air-raid shelter
than neglect his duty under the Children

(Scotland) Act 1995, to protect children
from public-opinion, press-gangs, panels,
politicians, perverts, piss-poor-parenting,
prefects, po-faced professionals, plook-
sookers and persons who drink polish.
The senior social worker is reading a report:
it says a senior police officer had sex with
his own daughter, aged nine, when his wife

became ill, because he was a strong Christian
and did not wish to break his marriage vows
by going outside the family. Her vaginal
walls are split and she may never have a
child of her own. The senior social worker
looks out of the window, and growls.

The Consultant's on the Phone Again

The Consultant's on the phone again,
a paragon, an ego the size of Ham-shire
which is where he hails from,
the Voice of God calling, in clipped tones,
for the taking of a Child Protection Order,
by me, of course, well, he can go and
raffle – doesn't want the blame, see,
of discharging a child back to an 'unsuitable
environment' – by which he means

> there's five more weans,
> the place is a tip,
> and the parents are always
> arguing

but, the legislation's plain – it says,
'significant harm' must be shown before
a Sheriff, only the medic's come up 'inconclusive',
and the surgeon's no sayin', along wi' him, that
the bruising's 'unexplained', so, he's going
to report me to my boss for not doing as I'm told,
by him! – well, if it gives them any pleasure –

I've more important things to do than bandy words
wi' him –

> like sending out three workers
> every day,
> and a coallie-dug,
> to shore the whole thing up.

Dog-dazer

Then there was the day the dog-dazer appeared,
unheralded, in a small cardboard box, on my desk,
sans instructions, just a plastic remote, like a fat
mobile phone before such things were invented,
with a button on, which emitted a noise that was
inaudible to the human ear but which made dogs
go demented, like cats getting scalded, ghettos
blasted, so we had a meeting just to make sure
and that's when Pattiann said she'd like to try it
out on her next visit to the Masons who we all knew
had a large Alsatian, called Sheeba, who looked at it
and growled while Pattiann pressed the button,
then Sheeba took it away to play with in a corner,
for the batteries had not been included.

Emergencies

Big Ronnie was on the phone, and the client
was crying and asking him what he was
going to do because she was holding
her child outside the window of her flat,
three-stories up, so Ronnie asked her
if she thought she would be strong enough
to hold on until the fire-brigade arrived,
but she thought not, so Big Ronnie
agreed this was tricky and he'd really
prefer more time to think about it, so
she agreed to bring the child back inside
and he'd phone her back in five minutes,
which he did, only to find that the child
had gone to play at a neighbour's instead.

Ordinary Everyday Madness

It's a bit like being in *Cracker*,
I suppose, only without the drama,

no chain-smoking, hard-drinking Fitz,
stalking the corridors of madness

for an hour, mostly his own – no,
what we get is 'normal', only more so,

a slightly obsessive need to fit in,
an outward show of routines, keeping

at bay generations of barely concealed
lunatic anxiety – though we don't go

into that, of course – what we concentrate on
is the mundane, the everyday realities,

accepting the fact that, when we go,
they will start talking to their bicycles.

Case Histories

destroying old case files, sifting through,
fragments, crumbling manila folders,
records of visits, tissue-thin carbon-copies,
letters, black Remington-type, scribbles,
notes, Dear Sir, I am, most grateful for,
Esquire, old paper smells, the Fifties,
hand-written pages, mental defectives,
illegitimate, slightly spastic, a typed
Children's Officer's Report, unsettled,
a deprived and demanding child, co-
habiting, nicely dressed, discharged,
admitted, I enclose a postal order for,
unkempt, ineligible, highly-strung,
treatment, manners, Miss   deleted

Process Recording

My first placement, 1971, Hamilton Burgh,
Joe Gillen asked me to do a process recording,
a detailed report on a visit I had made
which he reads then falls upon his knees, weeping.
'Shakespearean' he mumbled, between tears, gasps,
though more grim than Beckett I'd have thought,
a tale of love gone wry and told in fractured prose
and mind benumbing detail regarding a layette,
the putative father now missing, in prison, in fact,
and the young girl's father threatening to wring
his effing neck, and the DHSS not budging either,
saying the baby must survive, be living, for at least
six weeks before they'd give anything towards its
keep: Godot, alive, and waiting, in Hamilton.

Tutors

My rubicund, my full-bellied tutors, Morrison and
Carnegie, one rapier, one cutlass, one a smart-arse,
one on the look-out for vampires, the emotional sort.
They giggled, mock *roués* of 'the people processing
business', Morrison's phrase, how true that is today.
They cried 'On-guard!' then kicked you in the balls
to see if you had seen it coming, devised a hundred
ways of saying 'cabbage' just to change its meaning.
They paid a lone piper to crash Carnegie's lecture
on penal policy reform: 'Revenge And Retribution'.
He played a coronach. Morrison beamed, Carnegie
gleamed, like George Brown on a bender. I spied
Morrison years later, in a bookshop, and hid. But I
salute you now, my rubicund, my full-bellied tutors.

Social Workers On Tractors

Suddenly, we were genericised, overnight,
professionalised, mechanised and sat astride
our tractors, gleaming in the morning light,
mean-machines, tearing round the countryside
in our mini-skirts and sandals, clearing ground
like Aberdeenshire farmers clearing boulders
from parklands on angry Massey Fergusons,
draining swamps, marshlands, with the alligators
staring at us, strange creatures, strange vocabularies;
not by candlelight we led them, like fallen girls,
but straight through the barnyards, reformatories,
old workhouses, hospitals for the poor, gears
crashing, engines revving, hencoops scattering,
on and on we dragged them, heading for Jerusalem!

Ian Slater's Overcoat

Today, we have the Ian Slater overcoat,
genuine RSSPCC, large and roomy,
whole families once sheltered in its shade,
its inside pocket doubling as a place-of-safety,
if required, already signed by a magistrate,
which Ian carried about his person
just in case he came upon an emergency,
a drunken father, no food in the house,
a battered wife or wean; seven-hundred
and eighty-nine cases he had between Stirling
and Slamannan, and only himself, a female
assistant and a collie-dog to visit them, and,
every three months, a meeting held between the
whipper-in, school nurse and him, the cruelty man.

Mau-Mauing the Flak Catchers

Another incident in the unreported war
of manoeuvre between the establishment

and the underclass, a wee guy looking across
the desk at me in 1973 in Falkirk Burgh

social work department (side-chads, smoking
a roll-up – him, no me!) whose ancestors had

no doubt made the English feel unwelcome at
Bannockburn, anyway, he says, could he no

see somebody younger and maybe a bit better
looking (meaning the female student) so

when I said no he says that I wisnae gonnie
gie him fuckall, wis ah? and when I said no,

no even wi' a doctor's line, he just laughed,
and went back to wherever he had come fae.

Dancing With Big Eunice
Falkirk Burgh Social Work, 1973–5

Dancing with Big Eunice was,
I must confess,
a complete, knee-trembling experience.

She was a big girl, big and bonnie,
big in tights, and without oany.
She had a bum that come straight doon

from her hips and curved roond
like welded sheets of metal on the bow-sprits
of the *Queen Mary* – she was hairy –

where she needed to be – oan her heid! –
she had ringlets and curls, swirls and swurls,
and her eyes seemed to follow your crotch,

and wink Hi! as you walked by her room.
Her own walk was indescribable but went
something like – *Boom-Boom!*

During the day she typed up court reports,
made tea for perverts, and bad jokes,
and smiled at persons who fancied sheep

or wasted the time of the Bog Road police.
Eunice never wasted anybody's time.
She painted her eyes blue. Her lips

were red and redder grew, the more you
looked and the more she looked at you,
till they became like a great big pouting

nipple, or a marble, anyway, something
round and proud that you'd like to chew,
or maybe you'd like to chew you.

She had power over men, I ken, because
they told me. You know that picture
by Beryl Cook, *Ladies Night*, wi' yon

male stripper stretching oot his g-string
for these big dames to take a look?
Well, Eunice would just have reached

right in and grabbed it saying – Look!
Some'dy's broke the wee thing's neck!
O, she had a tongue, make no mistake,

and I'll tell you this, she used it for
mouth-to-mouth no hesitate, that's what
Eunice called   *a kiss!*

Her lips were soft, her breath was sweet,
you were in her grip, as her tongue unfurled
inside your cheek, and downward drove
towards your feet – where it turned and
growled, then upward hurled until it curled
around your waist, looking – no, licking –
for a label, then *Bang!* it started up and
whanged your y-fronts into double-spin,
no half-loads, no low-heat economic
settings here, just the steady beat of a
heavy-duty rinse, a throbbing pre-wash
tumble, and a superb blow-dry, a non-fast
coloured whirring, a chugg, a sough, that
sucked you up and hung you inside-out
to die, o my o my – nobody ever kissed you
better – except, perhaps, Wee Marion –
though she'll deny it to this day.

Care in the Community, 1974

I

Willie would sit in my office
    in Orchard Street
every Thursday after work,
    hurling hot-steel around
    the Carron Iron Works.

Fifty, he looked 98, cheeks clapped-in,
    no teeth, a mournful monk,
    a rabbit caught in headlights.

He'd been locked-up in a hospital for
    the insane for forty years, why?
    because he'd been 'a bad boy'

or so a doctor had told him, whose
    name he could not remember,
    no records, a long time ago, etcetera.

At our first meeting, I told him
    I was his new social worker
    and if there was anything
    he didn't understand, just ask.

I watched him sit in his jacket and cap,
    his haversack strapped on,
    like a First World War veteran
    waiting to go over the top.

His eyes lit upon the telephone on my
   desk and I heard him ask
   what it was and how did it work?
I said: when it rings you pick it up.

II

Willie got himself picked up a
   year later, at the bus-station,
   by Barbara, who'd asked him
   for a kiss.

She'd actually asked his pal first,
   Big Wull, but he didn't fancy it,
   but now all was fixed, they'd get
   married, have kids, which was what
he wanted to talk to me about: having sex.

We knew Barbara, of course,
   six children all adopted at birth.
   Now she worked and lived in an
   old folk's home in the Borders.

Willie told me how happy he was,
   that he might be a father. Of course,
   Barbara had had all the works
   taken out, years before.

So I said Willie, and Willie said yes,
   see Barbara, and Willie said yes,
   see on your wedding night, and
   Willie said yes, well, whatever
Barbara asks you to do, you do it.
   And Willie said yes.

III

The next hurdle to cross was Barbara's
    social worker, a spinster, but
    she agreed, even brought her old
    mother along to the reception.

All the office turned out and all went well
    until the Registrar could not get
    Willie to say his wedding vows,
    and so I, the best man, got him

to repeat them, after me: Danny, my
    senior, said that, legally,
    Barbara really married me.

Raymond

Raymond had two caseloads in 1976,
one he showed to me, the other he kept

in an 'open to duty' drawer in his desk,
mostly old guys in hostels, itinerants,

ex-psychiatric patients, old cons, war
veterans, who had no priority, who could

not compete with kids in residential homes,
and then there was Oswald, a sixteen-

year-old who kept getting kicked out by
his father, so Raymond gave him a sleeping

bag and food to sleep out in Callander
Park, it being summer. Raymond's face

went white when I told him I was leaving:
who else'll authorise the section 12s?

Best social worker I ever had, two for the
price of one.

Panels

Panels, the Children's Hearings, set up
as instruments of God by Lord Wheatley
to lead Scotland out of darkness in 1971
whereupon the number of children sent
away rocketed up, peaked in 1974, after which
Miss Gee retired, thank Christ, satiated, Chair
of Falkirk Burgh's Panel, an ex-headmistress,
everybody's granny, tho' the smell of burning
sulphur followed her about: Reporters now aim
for 'balance' in the Panels they provide – one a
flogger, one a new blood, and one in between –
fair enough, I say, though I would not let teachers
hear truancy cases, vested interests: but, overall,
they're miles ahead of public schoolboy Sheriffs.

Mrs McRobie

Caught sight of Davie McRobie bunking off school
    while sitting at the traffic-lights,
Graham's Road, saw his beatific face go from
    shock to delight when I,
his social worker, crunched into the tail-lights of a
    truck that had moved off
then stopped, saw the wee bastard tug his mate's
    coat, then run like fuck!

Mrs McRobie'd say: 'Whit kin ye dae, Mr Findlay?'
    Well, you might open the door
when I come up? – 'Aye, right enough.' She had five
    more, lived on fags and beer,
and wore a constant peeny, cleaned half the office
    blocks in Falkirk,
morning, noon and night – the Ice-Rink, Sheriff Court
    the Broo and Polis Stations,

locations not unfamiliar to her clan and brood although
    she never stole a thing in her life,
going from office space to office space like a coolie
    changing paddy-fields,
and giving her great lump of a man her pay packet,
    unopened: 'sair hodden doon'
her doctor might say, but as she told me herself, Tam,
    a liar and a thief,

was a bloody great lay! 'Whit kin ye dae, Mr Findlay?'
    'Aye, Mrs McRobie, right enough.'
So they took Davie away, and she gret every single day
    until they took him back.

Previous Cons

'I've a social background report to do on you.'
Tom Wallace, social worker, Falkirk Burgh, 1973

'I don't have a social background so you can fuck off.'
Jimmy Dee, who always took the alternative (3 months)

Danny Murphy and his neebs, PC 129 Fat Bob, are sat in
    their Panda at the Bog Road lights
when up creeps a lime green Ford Capri driven by Fergie
    McLaren McGee, 23 years old
and sallow, a bit like Huggy Bear, only darker, no having
    washed for a year
and banned for 30 years concurrent for taking and driving
    away without consent, tax disc
or benefit of clergy umpteen stolen cars, so Fergie tips
    his shades, jumps the lights
and hoors it away down South until he reaches Carlisle
    where he leaves a petrol-pump
attendant standing open mouthed when he decides not
    to pay by driving off,
despite having in the back-seat of the car, stolen that
    very day in Falkirk,
the proceeds of a robbery, then its a high-speed chase by
    the cops along the motorway,
heading for Bristol and an ex-Falkirk kind of Hole-in-the
    Wall gang, where Fergie thinks
he can claim, like John Wayne crossing the Rio Grande,
    sanctuary from prosecution.
O aye, and Fergie's on Probation to me, so he gets 2 years
    6 months consecutive added.

Tailgunner Parkinson

Old Tailgunner, they got him in the end,
of course, but what a hoot he was, urbane,
irreverent, his *New Society* columns chock
full of Romantic English prose, Shelley,
Byron, Blake, a wee *bon mot* then wham!
he got them, right in the rear-end, the bosses'
pomposity speared, penny-pinching schemes,
and Parky, pranging away as they flew past,
until he too got his in the tail-end, grassed
himself up too, in his own column, for
giving old cons cash to keep them out of prison
– and him a Probation Officer! Oh, they gave
him the bum's-rush, shot down for offending
market-forces, and endless mocking laughter.

A Client Remembers His Social Worker

for Peter Harris

Mr Harris always gave me good advice
never test-drive a Skoda
if you really want a Ford

avoid discounts of less than 10%
except for soft furnishings
and never buy furniture that's too big

for the room it's going into
you can never have too many gadgets
and things that whirr when you press them

never purchase anything
unless you've visited the factory twice
that's made them

seen one installed
and in full working-order
and sent back the warranty-guarantee slips

never jingle coins in Addiewell
and as for debt
as Mr Harris said avoid it

Here to read the meter, friend

We had no time for arse-lickers, apart from
the dedicated few, the tops of whose heads
you'd see whenever the Director opened
his gob, and rifted. No, our job was to care
and deal with those whom God and the
class-system made and coincidence
and the Poll-Tax had cast asunder, Life's
troubadours, Tommy Sheridan's crew,
mixed-in with victims and psychopaths,
whose doors you'd knock and sometimes hope
would be not there, not standing in the lobby
looking grim, rent book in one hand, meat
cleaver in the other: how tempting to have
called out then: here to read the meter, friend!

Notes Towards a Novel

I am a social worker, I hate people.
I work in Kafka's Castle,
Norman Bates delivers the mail.
The Waste Land is too joyous
to convey the dismay of those
who moil in the public good.
For this you must go back,
beyond irony, to the essay by
Emerson, *The Tragic*, 1844:

There are people who have
an appetite for grief, pleasure
is not strong enough and they
crave pain, mithridatic stomachs
which must be fed on poisoned
bread, natures so doomed that
no prosperity can soothe their
ragged and dishevelled desolation.

This may underestimate the case.
James Baldwin hated blackness
and whiteness, and the unbelievable
streets. He knew race doesn't matter,
class doesn't matter, sex doesn't
matter, nothing matters except your
humanity. I am a social worker, I
hate people and their appetites for grief.

The Client Said

The client said he was unaware
children were in the room
when he started rubbing his genitals
against the TV screen
because Gordon Brown came on
and he hates him.

The client said she took the children
to a friend in the early evening
before she starting drinking
then decided to dreep
from her second floor window
onto the bushes in the front garden.

The client said she burned
her left leg by pouring diesel
over it and setting it alight
but the pain got too much
so she thought if she drank
the rest it might knock her out.

Monday Morning Duty

It's Monday morning, again,
and, yes, I'm duty senior, so
I've read all the Emergency Referrals
– the Unrulies, the Self-Harms,
the Runaways, the Admissions, the
general round of Domestics and
Violations of the Peace – whit, in this dump?

Anyway, between the Forensic Medicals
and Joint Interviews, the ordinary mayhem
and clatters roond the heid, and the weans
found drunk in charge of their parents,
and the alcohol, crack and cocaine,
my eyes came upon this, a message from
a councillor, no, not a person offering therapy,

but someone definitely in need of some, yes,
a local *politicien*, worried, so he says,
about his constituents, who have found
some condoms in their back-garden – can we
please go round there straight away? Why –
to pick them up, make sure they're no his?
But now for some tea, and a read at the papers,

something to cheer me up, perhaps, the work
of the Scottish Government, Afghanistan.

Snap-shot

Heard it all now – just had an email –
the Corporate Manager, an Accountant
who used to be in charge of houses,
has been told by the Chief Executive,
an Accountant who used to be in charge
of wheelie-bins – which colour would you
like, madam? – who has told the Chief
Social Work Officer, who is now an
Accountant in charge of us, to offer up
a few ideas for a photo-shoot, now,

what this means is some grinning
councillor standing beside a wheel-chair,
not, I imagine, some child being forensically
examined for rape, a disaffected yob, an
ingrate, a doubly incontinent brain-damaged
inebriate, least of all, a drug-addict in prison
for injuring that child, because, you see,
and I suppose this is just a guess, but there
are just some things the great British public
just doesn't want to know about, or look at –

whether you photograph them, or not.

Shrubhill

Walking along the top corridor of Shrubhill,
Departmental HQ, coming along from
the opposite end towards me a heid bummer,
Gus Campbell, and as we approach
each other, like two old gun-slingers
in an ancient cowboy film, the corridor
completely empty apart from bosses coming
constantly in and out of each other's offices,
Gus suddenly raises his hand
while I slowly take an imaginary corner-kick
which Gus watches like a hawk, hanging
like Denis Law endlessly in the air,
until he too jumps into the air and heads
the imaginary ball through the doorway
of his secretary's office through which
he also disappears.

Work-to-Rule!

The strike was on, or rather, this
being social work, the work-to-rule

which the bosses and the council were
bending over backwards to ignore

tho' court reports weren't getting done
but ours was the only office holding out

so me and Jimmy Johnstone, the other
shop-steward, were shuttling between

workplace meetings and Roger Kent,
the Director, and Jimmy was getting

nervous which is bad when you've a voice
as loud as Jimmy's was, scared and angry

in turn, especially sitting in my car going
back to Craigmillar having just seen Roger.

'We're fucked,' Jim said, 'and some'dy's
going to get disciplined, me and you,

most like, so I'm going to tell them straight
this time, to give it up,' but Jimmy always

changed his mind and thundered out a Lenin
speech and so got carried by a cheering crowd

back to my car where he would groan and, yes,
repeat: 'We're really, really fucked this time.'

Police Report
Edinburgh 1567

On 5 September 1567, around two o'clock,
the marischall spotted a horse illegally
parked on the pavement at the Palace Gates,

nae lights displayed. He made his way,
unchallenged, into the Great Hall and came
upon the Queen dressed like a French

maid, carrying a lash. The subject, Knox,
wore a mask over his face and nothing
else, bar a nappy. The Queen said they

were rehearsing a new dance, the quadrille,
and he that they were going over a few
details on the deaths of David Riccio and

Cardinal Beaton, and tae eff aff, and had
they naethin better tae dae, in a mixture
of French, Greek and Latin. Knox ate the

ticket he was given. The Queen threatened
tae greet, and then started bawling 'Bothwell!
Bothwell!' who was then fetched from a

neighbour's the worse for wear. He boaked
on the marischall's vest and was taken into
custody for the violent breaking of wind.

They were all bound over the next day by
the magistrates and promised to be of good
behaviour for the rest of the Reformation.

Big Tam Says

Big Tam says they sold the jerseys, the Directors,
    caved in to the politicians, the bureaucrats,
and all for big pensions. Big Tam says we should have
    gone into BASW, the professional organisation,
instead of slaving in the unions, NALGO, UNISON,
    and all for the collective right of binmen
to work unlimited overtime in North Lanarkshire.
    Big Tam says if we'd our time over again
we'd take no prisoners, oppose the machinations
    of the corporate state, expose corruption
in low places, agitate for the professional assessment
    of need no matter the cost to the taxpayer.
Big Tam, I says, I thought we'd done that already:
    oh, aye, he says,
but next time we'll no be such Bloody Mr Nice Guys.

Managers

Managers, to adapt Lenin, were once
good men fallen among Fabians, but now
are vermin and should be taken out and re-
hired by Tesco. Managers knew their place,
came up through the ranks, knew what
the difference was between a big ball and
a wee one, protected their staff, let them
get on with the job, ran their committees,
told them that statistical returns, real or
imagined, had nothing to do with the price
of mince, that what was needed on the front
line was vocation, commitment, fosterhomes,
beds, good staff, more training, better culture,
more fosterhomes, good staff, real care taken.

No Problemo

Getting too old for this game,
holding onto an eight-year-old
spit-ball in the car-park
after a hearing that would not
send him home, so now he's
venting his wrath at the pavement
we are both now looking down on
my fourteen stone draped round
his shoulders while he questions
my parentage, my manhood
my professional credibility.

I feel his heart thumping against
my frame as we stand, or rather
crouch, in this foetal exchange
the world, and now me, weighed
round tiny Quasimodo-shoulders
until he breaks into a sob and rushes
forward to his carer demanding fish
for tea later. In the car not going home
he tells me that in three weeks time
the Panel will see it his way
and Celtic will win the League again

no problemo.

Child Protection Guidelines (the Latest)

Lift up the phone, when the caller says 'abuse',
panic, over-react, run out of the door shouting

hysterically, send two social workers also out
the door shouting hysterically, alert the police,

the zone paediatrician, ambulance service, fire-
brigade, health visitor, general practitioner,

midwife, Barnardo's, Tesco's, Dyno-Rod,
Visa, chief social work officer, child protection

register clerkess, her pal, the emergency duty
team, drug team, resources, criminal justice,

the Reporter to the Children's Hearing, the
Children's Hearing, the reviewing officer, the

area liaison coordinator's assistant for updating
the Scottish Executive's ongoing review of the

21st century social work's back-covering interim
consultative report, but, don't, repeat, don't

notify the parents, or ask a child anything, unless,
of course, you are accompanied by a police officer.

They Gave Us All Computers

they gave us all computers, oh,
ten years ago, one for each senior,

and one for every room of four, yes,
and they all sat there gathering dust

while we went on about our business,
visiting tents, undergrowths, until some

of the younger ones thought they'd look
up horoscopes, you know, Frankie Says,

on the Internet, so now they squat on us,
like great big toads hung about our necks

– croak! croak! – communications from the
boss – who sits in a secluded room eleven

miles away, and I'm the only one he'd
recognise, but the great fear is that they,

the clients, might start hacking back into
the system, start sending messages out

direct – Help, SOS, Shove-It – makes you
think, so now we stare at screens with

Orwell eyes, for we have seen the future
and, as Frankie said it would, it stinks

Social Welfare: a Fantasy in Scots

Fellow, you have broken our laws! Yes, your
Honour, but not before your laws had broken me.

William Thom
in *Justice Made Easy*
Tait's Magazine, Edinburgh, 1857

The gaberlunzie stood
on Waverley Steps
clinking, wet

the pennies in her blanket
jingle

(they say)

Ane cried the Meanistry o' Social Security
hae pished in thir mooths

(they mean the Statutes of Perth 1422–1524)

Maisters o' Correction sal entertain wasters, sornars,
overlayers or maisterful thiggers [all types of beggars]
harbouring on kirkmen or husbandmen [medieval taxpayers]
an bi a' correction necessary or sever, whipping or other
wise [excepting torture], jile or cleekit them – gif gear
enough [if they can pay] – or nail thir lugs til the trone
[or ony ither tree], or gif return, hing them. Coal-
maisters or Salt-maisters sal enthral ony sich wi siccar
[similar] powers, for the benefit o' thir wark.

the pennies in her blanket
jingle

Section 12

Section 12, the duty on local authorities to
promote social welfare, hailed as a revolutionary
clause. Santa Claus more like. It was what
the great Etzioni called a non-operational goal.
Too right, like the rest of social work, beyond
rational analysis, an act of faith, used in the early
days to employ community workers to organise
rent strikes, petition councils, fix drains, but it
couldn't last, councils paying rent arrears to
stop children coming into care. Then Big Fred
Edwards told the Scottish Office his staff *would*
pay out to striking miners to keep the weans fed.
One contradiction too many, I'm afraid, so when
the Tories began to eradicate poverty by selling off
council houses, we were told by the suits to only
pay a fiver per head per child – for lost giros, purses.

Swearing

Her wee eyes popped out, for once dumbstruck,
at what I'd said: haw you, button it,
and give your bum a rest, there's other folk
here wi' stuff to say apart frae you, aw right?
She'd been talking herself into Secure
and so out of the only place left in Scotland
prepared to hold her. You're no supposed to swear,
she said. And you're no supposed to stand
on staff car roofs either, like a bloomin' eejit!
The officer in charge then spoke jargon for quarter
of an hour. I said, you understand a word?
Nut, she said. Well neither did I, but the gist o' it
wis, dae it again and you'll be offski, you'll be ex-
here, aw right? She smiled. I'd made myself a friend.

Reading Files

when you read the file
before you've even met

and you see it all put down
in black and white

what they've done
and what's been done to them

stop in case you imagine
this great towering beast

with a huge fiery tongue
and glittering eyes

because in will come
this wee specky person

who wouldn't say boo
to the proverbial and you

will probably feel quids-in
and really rather amazed at

what your training didn't
quite prepare you for, again

Supervision

I was only supervised myself
for about ten minutes in 1973

when my senior read out the names
of my forty-five case files

tittering occasionally as he went
but I much prefer the honesty

of that to the ritualised exchange
formally written up and signed

so that if the shit-hitting-fan thing
occurs then no blame will attach

to the council or the agency
but as far as the worker goes

they will learn what we knew
right from the start: where the buck stops

An Early Social Work Training Film, Shot in 1973, starring Robert Mitchum

I

A mean wind wanders through the backcourt trash,[1]
an owl hoots, Vincent Price laughs, a police car
cruises past as the poem pans through *film-noir*
towards neglected lives, rats, psychopaths,
dwells on tenemented stairs, fag-ash,
then leaps to rub our backs on fictive air
that hangs like fetid breath, balderdash, haar
round Partick Cross, Maryhill, Alcatraz.
But who cares, for here comes Robert Mitchum,
social worker *extrordinaire*, a mug-shot,
and then he climbs the stair, finds a loose one,
then he's at the door he's looking for. He knocks.
A man with an axe appears, looking glum:
'Take them', he says, 'the wife, the weans, the lot.'

---

[1] first line of each verse same as first line of Edwin Morgan's *Glasgow Sonnets*

II

A shilpit dog fucks grimly by the close.
'He's doing what The Social does to us,'
the axe-man says. Bob sighs. 'I'll call the fuzz.
Axeman, you're not my scene. Adios.'
And then down crumbling stairs Bob Mitchum goes,
the wife and the weans following until Angus,
the director, calls 'Cut! Bob! Fabulous!
We caught their ghastly faces half-exposed.'
Bob yawns. 'Why don't Probation carry guns?
Can I not at least shoot the dog, the weans?
This social work's all crap, they talk like nuns
and fill out forms and make expenses claims
and bleat about the dead-beats, bad-guys, huns.
Who gives a shit for bums, the shit-for-brains?'

III

'*See a tenement due for demolition?*
Me, I'd hang the mayor from it'n call the press,
then network deals. When *Fathers For Injustice*
stage a protest, we shoot them: Intermission.
We televise the Beatles signing a petition
to re-house everyone in Scotland, yes,
who needs one, the wives, the weans and the dis-
possessed, or we start dropping politicians
on their heads, one by one. We dramatise!
Social workers'd distribute guns to those
least fit to use them. Man, we'd organise
the clients, collectivise human rights, pose
vital questions like: what's your babies' lives
worth, shitheads? And all in one take, amigos.'

IV

Down by the brickworks you get warm at least.
Axeman pauses, lights another cigarette.
Bob looks glum, he's heard it all before, would bet
a pound to a bird's-shite Axeman'll be creased
by noon in some crummy joint, Rab C Nesbitt's
most like, 'victim' boaked all across his vest,
kept warm by whisky-chasers. 'Jesus Christ,
Axeman,' Bob explodes, 'what about the weans? Forget
the booze, the greeting in your drinks. Be a man,
my son, or you will die a low-life, loser,
bum!' The Axeman meets Bob's gaze. 'But ah am
a bum,' Axe says, 'and, yes, by god, a slaver,
but never count me out, Bob, for I can turn
my life round now, if I model your behaviour.'

V

'Let them eat cake', made no bones about it.
'If Marie Antoinette'd lived in Govan
she'd have lost her fear of tumbrels even'
– Bob Mitchum tells the youth, the paralytic –
'it's not cool, you shit-for-brains should shove it,
look for jobs, apprenticeships, education,
stand up for human rights and join the unions.'
Then Axeman sobers up, kicks the habit,
gets his wife and weans back, becomes a Jehovah's
Witness, and enters social work training,
becomes a Director of Sure Start, a
non-profit-making organisation – since waning.
Bob Mitchum smiles, unsuspecting, Mrs Thatcher's
not yet ridden into town and shot his happy ending.

Three Hundred Spartans

How can I express the unutterable echtness,
the dree, Three Hundred Spartans deid, and

me here on the brig on ma lane: think TS
Eliot, the hot gates, knee-deep, bitten, fought,

in the salt marsh, heaving a cutlass, eyeless,
think *Scream 3*, *Edward Scissorhands*, think

Addiewell, ach, but who now knows, or cares,
what the difference was between a hawk and a

handsaw, most never could, most just did
what they were told, social workers, I mean,

no the clients, Jeesus! Behave yoursel'! –
but some, a few, did make a difference to

those between a rock and a hard place; now
it's all fear, a driven pack outside and in here

a crowd of no-risk-takers, hacking holes in me,
aye, me! – ma vest – the last bleeding Trojan.

MBAS

We used to read Biestek on non judgemental
relationships, Hollis and Pearlman,
Maslow on hierarchical needs,
the choice between fight or flight, Erikson,
self determination, client centred practice
and to what extent we are, or ought to be,
agents of social change or social control,
ho hum, that old one, reform or revolution,
and so it went on, ad infinitum.
When the state became this massive casino
our finest began taking MBAS in accountancy
and brown-nosing. Now the banks have bust
we may have to concentrate once more on
some of the old stuff: saving, the price of mince.

Bob Purvis

I see Bob Purvis died, a lovely man.
He ran the old Family Service Unit,
Castlemilk, when I was a student there,
1972. He chain-smoked, clicked his teeth
and talked and talked, told endless stories,
how debt-collectors nailed folk to the floor,
'cos that's still the drill round here, you know,
the syllables of 'drill' hung in the air
until the knee-caps froze, and then he clicked
his teeth once more and looked at you, and grinned.
A young wife told me that when her man got drunk
he pissed into the chest-of-drawers instead of
walking to the loo, and what should she do?
I asked if I could talk to him, and she laughed.

Baby P

that photograph
your face smeared with chocolate
to hide the bruising

the wary look
the expressionless gaze
we are always told to look out for

though it will not stand up in court
by itself
but the question is who took it

a neighbour
a nursery nurse
taken in as you were not

by the mother
the cunning lodger
the moronic boyfriend

certainly not the paparazzi
grown tired of snapping
endless Royal drawers

getting in and out of
magazines
the tabloid press

nor the chaps and chapesses
no longer down at
Council HQ

their eyes no longer kept
firmly fixed on
the bottom line

their desks cleared
their master's voice
now boldly ringing in their ears

that photograph

haunting me
haunting you
haunting them

Brandon Muir
the radio phone-in

where were the social workers
where were the grandparents
where were the friends and neighbours

exterminate the drug addicts
sterilise the drug addicts
stop the methadone programmes

what about the alcoholics
what about the criminals
what about the government

and
our final caller
stuff the do-gooders

Tragedy

Tragedy, nothing new, old as death, dogs all
our footsteps, open any newspaper,
the jokers of the press, the editorial
reaching out for metaphors like 'human nature'
which does not exist, my friend, but dusted off,
may do to swell the note of righteous indignation,
while some poor clod, fifty of a caseload and half
way down the food chain, submits their resignation,
yet they're the lucky ones – their nightmare's over;
we who remain still have to read the Enquiry Report
written by some bourgeois, some big-shot lawyer,
who's never taken kids away, cleaned up snot,
awaited outcomes or thrown themselves upon
the fetid breath, the so-called court of 'public opinion'.

We go to our posts in the morning

We go to our posts in the morning,
our desk-tops, our cell-phones,
the daily rituals, the unwrapping of forms,

visits to clients, perhaps, or
more likely, the courts and the hearings,
then lunch, the anarchy of duty,

the wailings and gnashings, the witherings
and scorns of the inept and maladjusted,
and those just the councillors,

and those that lack insight, sometimes
called managers, while we, the workers,
upborne only by the example of the

local constabulary, those soldiers of
enlightenment, who have learned over
centuries how to combine authority with

respect, how to smile and say 'sir' and
'madam' and 'no', even to the most
paralytic and rat-arsed of our citizens,

and then to go home.

Pelt

I no longer have skin but pelt,
like some great rugged animal,
wintering out beneath the snow line,
formidable, while the smell of musk
hangs in the air and seasons change,
yet my coat remains impervious,
which is what it was made for,
to bear whatever human nature scorns
and makes others shudder no longer
bothers me, like some great elk, I am
fashioned by the elements of its domain;
forests wave around me, antlers snag, yet
still pass through, a way found where none
seemed possible: I yawn, a tree falls, it rains.

Mollycoddling

My mother, ninety-three,
blames me and my kind
for mollycoddling the feckless.

She watches *Oprah* for ammunition,
occasionally saying 'Ye'd just like tae
shake them!' I say I know the feeling.

My mother was honed from birth
to almost death by work and soap
and water flung on rock-face

and hearth like pounding surf
on iron-black metallic range
before which she knelt and cursed

sweating and scrubbing and now
she sits like some old steam-engine
balefully eying the slope

the distance between herself
and the imitation fire-place
on which dust is settling.

She stares out at the weeds through
double-glazed windows and shouts
'Damned cats, shitting on my geraniums!'

Desks

Social workers cover their desks with photographs
of kids they have in care

hang their vivid red blue and green paintings up
plaster their walls with posters

though none of them from olden times
that tennis player scratching her bum

or banners from ancient demos
peace marches and strikes

with captions like 'support your local police force:
beat yourself up'

mostly photos of previous Team Nights Out
dried up plants, banana skins

the entrails of a three weeks late social background
report – nearly done – and the telephone ringing

A Silver Grey One

Clearing out my desk I came upon
an old claw-hammer, a keep-sake,
from a distraught mother, trying
to stop us taking her son away
because the Panel said so. I didn't
know the case, but being back-up
senior, I helped the worker out.
Up three flights, his case was packed
and all seemed fine until she
disappeared and then came back
with this thing she broke coal with,
and we were trapped between her
and the door, so I grabbed it fast
and pinned her to the wall while they
squeezed past, but she somehow
got my bunnet and threw it off
the landing. We watched it soar,
I see it still, a silver grey one.

Alan Finlayson

The great Alan Finlayson, Rumpole
of the Reporter's Department, Lothian Region,
a brilliant wee barrel-voiced solicitor,
full of wit and humour and lawyer's lore
yet deep-down serious about justice.
'Guidelines?' he intoned, 'so that social workers
will know what my job is? Surely not? Just
say "phone Finlayson", he'll know if there's a
case to answer.' Too right he did. All this guff
about 'interagency decision-making',
a fancy way of saying 'pass-the-buck'
back to social work, never any 'closure',
polis talking like social workers, consultants
like polis: give me Alan Finlayson, any time.

Sonnet Frae the Social Works

Wir clapt-oot tramp steamers
doonladen wi' ores, subs frae the Indies,
electric bar fires, wir tubs fu' o' dreamers
but deep in wir holds thir's urgent supplies,
unguents frae the Orient and the Azores,
the Isthmus o' Panama, Orkney an' Mars,
in th'Isthmus o' Greenock wir knockin' doon doors
wi' breidplants an' incense, baked beans an' spam,
wir lambasted by trade winds, becalm'd, submarined
wir mendin' propeller blades an' doon-broke camshafts,
wir Hepburn and Bogart oan the *African Queen*
in wir semmits and vests cryin' *Come-oan, Get-aft!*
Abin us the war cloods ominous form,
ablow us wir vessels puff intil the storm.

On Retiral from Public Service

I've left my Humphrey Bogart poster
looking down on six Scottish Colourists

hanging on my wall, and although
John Cleese's *Ministry of Silly Walks*

has gone, the bowler-hatted business-men
of René Magritte rain on, remorselessly,

from the heavens, and whoever pinned
Laurel & Hardy to my office door,

holding onto each other for comfort on
some precipitous ledge, with the legend

   – Oh No! He's Duty-Senior Again! –
has kindly removed it, now that Elvis

has gone, has finally left the building,
for good, for ever   *singing*

Luath Press Limited
committed to publishing well written books worth reading

LUATH PRESS takes its name from Robert Burns, whose little collie Luath (*Gael.*, swift or nimble) tripped up Jean Armour at a wedding and gave him the chance to speak to the woman who was to be his wife and the abiding love of his life. Burns called one of 'The Twa Dogs' Luath after Cuchullin's hunting dog in Ossian's *Fingal*. Luath Press was established in 1981 in the heart of Burns country, and now resides a few steps up the road from Burns' first lodgings on Edinburgh's Royal Mile. Luath offers you distinctive writing with a hint of unexpected pleasures.

Most bookshops in the UK, the US, Canada, Australia, New Zealand and parts of Europe either carry our books in stock or can order them for you. To order direct from us, please send a £sterling cheque, postal order, international money order or your credit card details (number, address of cardholder and expiry date) to us at the address below. Please add post and packing as follows: UK – £1.00 per delivery address; overseas surface mail – £2.50 per delivery address; overseas airmail – £3.50 for the first book to each delivery address, plus £1.00 for each additional book by airmail to the same address. If your order is a gift, we will happily enclose your card or message at no extra charge.

Luath Press Limited
543/2 Castlehill
The Royal Mile
Edinburgh EH1 2ND
Scotland
Telephone: 0131 225 4326 (24 hours)
Fax: 0131 225 4324
email: sales@luath.co.uk
Website: www.luath.co.uk